Successful Effective New Habits Book

Change Habits for Wealth Building,
Emotional Intelligence
& Weight Loss Guide
by Brian Mahoney

Table of Contents

Introduction: The Power of Habits

Chapter 1 Why We Form Bad Habits

Chapter 2 Breaking the Cycle

Chapter 3 The Cost of Staying the Same

Chapter 4 Rewiring Eating Habits

Chapter 5 Movement as a Lifestyle

Chapter 6 Mind over Plate

Chapter 7 Breaking the Cycle of Overspending

Chapter 8 Building Financial Discipline

Chapter 9 The Wealth Mindset

Chapter 10 Understanding Emotional Intelligence

Chapter 11 Replacing Reactivity with Response

Chapter 12 Strengthening Relationships through EQ

Chapter 13 Habit Stacking for Success

Chapter 14 The Role of Accountability

Chapter 15 Celebrating Milestones

Conclusion

Glossary of Terms

Disclaimer

The information presented in this book is for educational and informational purposes only. While the strategies and advice offered are based on widely recognized principles of personal development, health, finance, and emotional intelligence, they are not intended to serve as professional medical, financial, or psychological advice.

Before making any significant changes to your diet, exercise routine, or financial practices, it is strongly recommended that you consult with a licensed professional, such as a doctor, financial advisor, or therapist, to ensure that the steps you take are appropriate for your individual circumstances.

The author and publisher are not responsible for any injuries, financial losses, or emotional distress that may occur as a result of implementing the information provided in this book. Any action you take based on the content of this book is done at your own risk.

Every effort has been made to ensure the accuracy of the information in this book, but the author and publisher make no guarantees regarding the results you may experience. Success is ultimately determined by your individual commitment, circumstances, and consistency in applying the strategies discussed.

By using this book, you acknowledge and agree to these terms.

Introduction:
The Power of Habits

Habits are the building blocks of our daily lives. From the moment you wake up to the time you go to bed, much of what you do is driven by automatic routines rather than conscious decisions. These habits can either propel you toward success or keep you stuck in cycles of frustration, self-doubt, and missed opportunities.

This book is about harnessing the transformative power of habits to reverse those that don't serve you and replace them with ones that lead to a healthier body, a wealthier future, and stronger emotional intelligence. By understanding the science of habits and applying practical strategies, you can fundamentally change the trajectory of your life.

1. The Invisible Force Shaping Your Life

Habits operate like an autopilot system, guiding your actions without requiring constant thought or effort. They are efficient, saving mental energy by allowing you to perform tasks without overthinking. However, this same efficiency can be detrimental when bad habits take root.

Examples of Habits' Power:

    Positive Habits: Brushing your teeth, exercising regularly, or sticking to a budget.

    Negative Habits: Mindless snacking, procrastinating, or overspending.

Your habits don't just shape your daily routine; they determine the results you see in your health, finances, relationships, and emotional well-being.

Key Insight:

Small habits, repeated consistently, have a compounding effect over time. A seemingly insignificant behavior today can lead to significant outcomes months or years down the line.

Reflection Task:

Identify one habit, good or bad, that has significantly impacted your life. Write down how it has shaped where you are today.

2. Why We Struggle to Break Bad Habits

Reversing bad habits can feel like an uphill battle, and there's a reason for that: habits are deeply ingrained in your brain. The cycle of cue, routine, and reward forms a powerful loop that becomes difficult to break.

The Habit Loop:

Cue: A trigger that initiates the habit.

Routine: The action you take in response to the cue.

Reward: The benefit or relief you gain, which reinforces the behavior.

Bad habits are often fueled by immediate rewards, even if the long-term consequences are harmful. For example:

Overeating provides instant comfort but leads to weight gain.

Impulse purchases bring temporary excitement but harm your finances.

Reacting emotionally to conflicts feels cathartic but damages relationships.

Reflection Task:

Think of a bad habit you struggle with. Identify its cue, routine, and reward.

3. The Potential for Transformation

The good news is that habits are not set in stone. They are patterns, and patterns can be changed with the right approach. By understanding how habits work and learning to consciously replace them, you can turn destructive cycles into empowering ones.

Consider This:

Instead of reaching for junk food when stressed, you can train yourself to go for a walk or practice deep breathing.

Instead of avoiding financial planning, you can establish a habit of tracking your expenses daily.

Instead of reacting impulsively in emotionally charged situations, you can learn to pause and choose a thoughtful response.

The goal isn't to eliminate habits—it's to build better ones. By doing so, you gain control over your actions and create a life aligned with your aspirations.

Action Step:

Write down one bad habit you want to reverse and brainstorm a healthier habit to replace it.

4. Why This Book Matters

This book is your guide to transformation. It's about more than breaking bad habits—it's about reclaiming your power to shape your life intentionally. Whether your goal is to lose weight, gain financial stability, or strengthen your relationships, the strategies in this book will equip you to:

Identify the habits holding you back.

Understand the underlying triggers and rewards driving them.

Replace destructive patterns with positive, sustainable behaviors.

What You'll Learn:

The psychology and science of habits.

Practical techniques for rewiring your behavior.

How to create a system of accountability and celebrate progress.

Through this process, you'll uncover your potential to not just achieve goals, but to build a life of purpose, discipline, and fulfillment.

5. Your Journey Begins Here

Breaking bad habits and building better ones is a journey, not an overnight fix. It requires commitment, self-awareness, and resilience. But the rewards are life-changing. Imagine a version of yourself who:

Wakes up energized and confident, knowing you're making choices that support your health.

Feels in control of your finances and excited about your financial future.

Navigates relationships with empathy, patience, and emotional intelligence.

This transformation is possible—and it starts with one small step at a time.

Final Task:

Set an intention for this journey. Write down one specific area of your life you're committed to improving through the strategies in this book.

Closing Thoughts on the Power of Habits

Habits are not just actions—they're expressions of who you are and who you are becoming. By taking charge of your habits, you take charge of your destiny. This book will serve as your roadmap to reversing bad habits and unlocking the healthier, wealthier, and emotionally intelligent version of yourself that's waiting to emerge.

Let's begin.

Chapter 1:
Why We Form Bad Habits

Instructor's Guide to Understanding and Addressing Bad Habits

Welcome! You're here because you recognize that some of your habits are holding you back, and that's a brave and powerful first step. Let's start by understanding why these habits exist—because knowing the "why" gives us the tools to change them.

1. What Are Habits?

Habits are automatic actions your brain has programmed to save energy. Think of brushing your teeth or tying your shoes—you don't have to think about them; they just happen. That's the good side of habits.

The challenge is when habits turn against you, like scrolling social media for hours or overeating when stressed. These are patterns your brain learned because, at some point, they made you feel better or solved a problem, even if just temporarily.

2. Understanding Your Habit Loop

To fix bad habits, you must first understand how they work. Every habit has three parts:

    Cue (Trigger): This is what sets your habit into motion. It could be an emotion, a time of day, or even a smell.

        Example: You feel bored at work.

    Routine (Behavior): This is the action you take in response to the cue.

Example: You grab a bag of chips to snack on.

Reward: This is the payoff that reinforces the behavior, even if it's short-lived.

Example: You feel a brief sense of pleasure from eating the chips.

Your Task:

Think of one bad habit you'd like to change. Write down:

The cue that triggers it.

The routine you follow.

The reward you get.

3. Why Do Bad Habits Stick?

Bad habits stick because they give you something you want—usually, instant gratification. Let's break it down:

You feel stressed (cue), so you binge-watch TV (routine) to feel relaxed (reward).

The problem? That "reward" is temporary and doesn't address the root issue—your stress.

Bad habits also thrive in environments that make them easy. Think about it: if junk food is always in your house, it's harder to avoid. Or if your phone is within reach, scrolling becomes automatic.

Your Task:

Spend a day observing yourself. What habits happen without you thinking? What triggers them? Write down as much as you can.

4. Are You Reinforcing Your Bad Habits?

Sometimes, we reinforce bad habits without realizing it. For example:

    Telling yourself, "I always fail at dieting," gives your brain an excuse to stop trying.

    Using phrases like, "I'm just a night owl," can keep you from building a productive morning routine.

Here's the truth: the stories you tell yourself shape your habits. If you see yourself as someone who can't change, your habits will reflect that.

Your Task:

Write down any labels you've given yourself (e.g., "I'm bad with money"). Challenge them by asking: "Is this really true, or is it just a habit of thinking?"

5. The Hidden Costs of Bad Habits

Bad habits aren't just annoying—they come at a price.

    Health: Procrastinating on exercise or eating poorly affects your body.

    Wealth: Overspending or failing to save drains your financial stability.

    Emotions: Reacting instead of reflecting can harm your relationships and self-esteem.

Ask yourself:

How is this habit holding me back?

What would my life look like if I replaced it with something better?

Your Task:

Write down one way a bad habit is costing you in each area: health, wealth, and emotions. Be honest with yourself.

6. Let's Start Small: Your First Step to Change

To change a bad habit, you don't need to fix everything at once. Start by understanding one habit and its triggers. For now, focus on becoming aware.

Keep a Journal: For one week, jot down when your bad habit happens, what triggered it, and how you felt afterward.

Ask "Why?": Dig deep. Why do you turn to this habit? What need are you trying to meet?

Remember: bad habits are often just solutions to unmet needs. Once you understand the need, you can find healthier ways to meet it.

Chapter 2:
Breaking the Cycle of Bad Habits

Welcome back! By now, you've taken the first step: understanding the why behind your bad habits. Great work. Now, let's shift gears and talk about how to break free from those cycles and start creating lasting change. This chapter will be all about strategies—simple, practical, and effective.

1. Recognize the Power of Awareness

The first step in breaking any habit is shining a light on it. Many bad habits thrive in the dark—they happen so automatically that we don't even realize we're doing them.

Imagine this: You walk into your kitchen and, without thinking, grab a snack. Why? Because it's a habit. But what if you paused and asked yourself, "Am I actually hungry?" That moment of awareness is where change begins.

Your Task:

For the next week, use this simple habit interruption technique:

When you catch yourself about to engage in a bad habit, pause.

Ask yourself:

What am I feeling right now?

Why am I about to do this?

Is there a healthier way to handle this moment?

2. Replace, Don't Remove

Here's a truth: habits are hard to "break," but they can be replaced. Your brain doesn't like a void. If you try to stop a bad habit without putting something else in its place, you're more likely to revert back.

Example:

Old Habit: Grabbing a sugary soda every afternoon.

Replacement Habit: Reaching for sparkling water or herbal tea instead.

Notice you're still honoring the craving for a drink but with a healthier choice.

Your Task:

Pick one bad habit you want to work on this week. Write down:

The habit you want to replace.

A positive alternative that meets the same need.

Commit to practicing the replacement for one week.

3. Control Your Environment

Many habits are influenced by your surroundings. If your environment supports your bad habit, it's like trying to swim upstream. Change your environment, and you make it easier to change your behavior.

Examples:

Problem: You overeat junk food.

Solution: Remove junk food from your house and stock up on healthy snacks.

Problem: You procrastinate by watching TV.

Solution: Keep your remote in a drawer and place a book or your work materials on the couch instead.

Your Task:

Pick one habit that's tied to your environment. Then:

Identify the trigger in your surroundings.

Change that part of your environment to make the habit harder to do.

4. Use the Power of Small Wins

Big, sweeping changes often fail because they're overwhelming. Instead, aim for small, manageable victories that build momentum over time.

Example:

Instead of saying, "I'm going to work out for an hour every day," start with just 5 minutes.

If you want to cut back on screen time, start by reducing it by 10 minutes a day.

The key is consistency. Small wins lead to big changes.

Your Task:

Identify one "small win" you can work on today. What's one tiny action that moves you in the right direction? Write it down and commit to doing it every day for a week.

5. Use Accountability to Stay on Track

Let's face it: changing habits is hard to do alone. Having someone to keep you accountable can make all the difference.

Examples of Accountability Tools:

  Buddy System: Find a friend or family member who can check in on your progress.

  Public Commitments: Share your goals with others—this creates external pressure to follow through.

  Tracking Progress: Use a habit tracker app or a simple calendar to mark each day you stick to your goal.

Your Task:

Pick an accountability method that works for you. Write it down and set it up today.

6. Practice Self-Compassion

Breaking a habit isn't a straight path. You'll have setbacks, and that's okay. The goal isn't perfection—it's progress.

When you slip, avoid beating yourself up. Instead, ask:

What triggered this?

How can I prepare better for next time?

Treat yourself with the same kindness you'd offer a friend.

Your Task:

Write a self-compassion statement you can use when you slip. Example:

"It's okay to have setbacks. I'm learning and improving every day."

7. Breaking the Cycle in Action

Here's a summary of the steps you'll take to break your bad habit:

Recognize it: Build awareness of the habit.

Replace it: Choose a healthier alternative.

Restructure your environment: Remove triggers and temptations.

Start small: Focus on consistent, manageable actions.

Stay accountable: Get support and track your progress.

Be kind to yourself: Learn from setbacks and keep moving forward.

In the next chapter, we'll take a deeper dive into the hidden costs of bad habits and how they impact your health, wealth, and emotional well-being. For now, focus on observing, replacing, and practicing these strategies.

Remember, change is a process, and you're doing great!

Chapter 3: The Cost of Staying the Same

Welcome to Chapter 3! So far, we've discussed why habits form and how to start breaking the cycle. But let's pause for a moment and ask ourselves: What happens if I don't change?

This isn't about scaring you—it's about helping you understand the true cost of staying stuck in bad habits. Once you see how much you stand to lose, you'll feel even more motivated to create a better future.

1. The Health Costs of Bad Habits

Bad habits take a toll on your body over time. The damage may not show immediately, but over months and years, the consequences can add up.

Common Health Costs:

   Poor Diet Choices: Can lead to weight gain, heart disease, diabetes, and fatigue.

   Lack of Exercise: Weakens your muscles, decreases your stamina, and contributes to chronic illnesses.

   Stress and Poor Sleep Habits: Lower your immune system, increase blood pressure, and leave you feeling mentally drained.

The Reality Check:

Imagine being 5, 10, or 20 years into the future. How will these habits impact your physical health? Will you have the energy to enjoy life, travel, or play with your children or grandchildren?

Your Task:

Write down one bad health habit you currently have. Next, write a short description of how it might affect you if you continue it for the next 10 years.

2. The Financial Costs of Bad Habits

Bad habits can quietly drain your wallet. Think about those daily expenses or impulsive spending decisions—how much are they really costing you?

Examples of Financial Costs:

   Daily Coffee Runs or Takeout: $5 a day may not seem like much, but over a year, that's nearly $2,000.

   Impulse Purchases: Clothes, gadgets, or subscriptions you don't use can add up fast.

   Missed Opportunities: Spending instead of saving or investing limits your financial growth.

The Reality Check:

Imagine where your finances could be if you redirected even a portion of your spending into savings or investments.

Your Task:

Review your recent expenses. Identify one habit or expense you could cut back on. Write down how much you'd save in a month and a year by changing this one habit.

3. The Emotional Costs of Bad Habits

Bad habits don't just affect your body and bank account—they also weigh on your mind and heart.

Emotional Costs:

   Low Self-Esteem: Repeatedly failing to change can make you feel defeated or stuck.

   Damaged Relationships: Neglecting loved ones, poor communication, or reactivity can strain your connections.

   Mental Overload: Stress from procrastination or unfinished tasks can leave you feeling overwhelmed.

The Reality Check:

What would your emotional life look like if you replaced one bad habit with a healthy, uplifting one? Could you be more confident, less stressed, or closer to the people you care about?

Your Task:

Think of one bad habit that negatively impacts your emotions or relationships. Write down how your life would improve emotionally if you overcame it.

4. Opportunity Costs: What Are You Missing Out On?

Every bad habit steals time and energy that could be spent on something more meaningful. Let's consider:

   Time: Procrastination, binge-watching, or mindless scrolling could be used to learn new skills, build relationships, or work on your dreams.

Energy: Bad habits drain mental and physical energy, leaving you too exhausted to pursue your goals.

The Reality Check:

Ask yourself: What could you achieve if you reclaimed just one hour a day from your bad habits?

Your Task:

Write down one big goal you've been putting off. Now calculate how much time you'd save each week by cutting back on one time-wasting habit.

5. The Cost of Regret

Regret is one of life's heaviest burdens. Imagine looking back years from now and wishing you had made different choices. The good news? You're here, and you have the power to change.

The Reality Check:

Think about the future version of yourself. What advice would they give you about the habits you need to change today?

Your Task:

Write a letter from your "future self" to your current self, explaining how your life improved once you started breaking your bad habits.

6. Turning Awareness Into Action

By now, you've reflected on how bad habits are impacting your health, wealth, and emotions. Let's channel that awareness into motivation:

Write a statement about why you want to change. Example:

"I want to feel energized and confident in my body so I can play with my grandchildren without getting tired."

"I want to build wealth so I can retire comfortably and support my family."

Final Thoughts

Staying the same has a price—one that grows bigger the longer you wait. But here's the good news: every step you take today, no matter how small, reduces that cost and moves you closer to the life you want.

In the next chapter, we'll explore how to reverse specific bad habits, starting with your physical health. For now, stay focused on what's at stake and use it as fuel for change. You're doing amazing work—keep going!

Chapter 4: Rewiring Eating Habits

Food is one of the most powerful influences on your physical health, energy, and overall well-being. Yet, eating habits are also some of the most challenging to change. Why? Because food is tied to our emotions, routines, and even our social lives. In this chapter, we'll explore how to rewire your eating habits to align with your health goals, without feeling deprived or overwhelmed.

1. Why We Struggle With Eating Habits

Eating habits are often influenced by:

   Emotions: Stress, boredom, or sadness can drive emotional eating.

   Convenience: Fast food and processed snacks are easy but often unhealthy.

   Environment: Unhealthy options may be more accessible than nutritious ones.

   Learned Behavior: Many eating patterns stem from childhood, such as finishing everything on your plate or using food as a reward.

The key to rewiring your eating habits is recognizing these patterns and learning how to interrupt them.

2. Start With Awareness

The Food Diary Exercise:

Before you can change your eating habits, you need to understand them. For one week, keep a food diary. Write down:

What you eat (everything, even snacks).

When you eat (time of day).

Why you eat (hunger, stress, boredom, celebration, etc.).

How you feel afterward (satisfied, guilty, energized, etc.).

Why This Works:

This exercise reveals patterns, such as eating out of habit rather than hunger or choosing unhealthy options when stressed. Awareness is the first step to change.

3. Break the Emotional Eating Cycle

Emotional eating often starts with a trigger—stress, boredom, or sadness. The key is to replace the behavior with something healthier.

Steps to Break Emotional Eating:

Identify the Trigger: Pause and ask, "Am I truly hungry, or is this emotional?"

Interrupt the Cycle: Choose an alternative activity, like walking, journaling, or calling a friend.

Practice Mindful Eating: When you eat, focus on the flavors, textures, and enjoyment of the food. This reduces overeating and builds satisfaction with smaller portions.

4. Plan Your Meals With Intention

Healthy eating starts with planning. When you have nutritious options readily available, it's easier to make better choices.

Steps to Plan Successfully:

Meal Prep: Set aside time each week to prepare healthy meals or snacks.

Stock Your Kitchen: Keep nutritious foods like fruits, vegetables, whole grains, and lean proteins on hand.

Pre-Portion Snacks: Instead of eating straight from the bag, divide snacks into single servings to avoid overeating.

Schedule Meals: Eat at consistent times to reduce mindless grazing.

Your Task:

Plan one day of meals and snacks. Write it down and commit to following it.

5. Control Your Environment

Your surroundings play a huge role in your eating habits. If junk food is within easy reach, it's harder to resist.

Steps to Create a Healthy Eating Environment:

   Out of Sight, Out of Mind: Keep unhealthy snacks out of sight or out of the house.

   Visual Cues: Display healthy options like fruit or nuts on the counter.

   Smaller Plates: Use smaller plates to control portions and avoid overeating.

   Distraction-Free Meals: Avoid eating in front of screens to stay mindful.

Your Task:

Make one change to your environment today that supports healthier eating.

6. Build Better Habits, One Step at a Time

Changing eating habits doesn't mean overhauling your entire diet overnight. Focus on small, manageable steps.

Examples of Small Wins:

    Swap soda for water or tea.

    Add a serving of vegetables to your dinner.

    Choose whole grains instead of refined carbs.

    Pack your lunch instead of eating out.

Your Task:

Pick one small change to your eating habits. Practice it consistently for one week before adding another change.

7. Redefine "Treats" and Rewards

Food is often used as a reward, but this can reinforce unhealthy habits. Instead, find non-food ways to celebrate or comfort yourself.

Examples of Non-Food Rewards:

    A relaxing bath.

    Buying a new book or outfit.

    Taking time to enjoy a hobby.

Your Task:

Write down three non-food rewards you'll use to celebrate your progress.

8. Balance, Not Perfection

Healthy eating isn't about perfection—it's about balance. It's okay to enjoy your favorite foods occasionally. The key is moderation.

Tips for Balance:

Follow the 80/20 Rule: Eat nutritious foods 80% of the time, and allow indulgences for the other 20%.

Practice Portion Control: You can enjoy dessert without going overboard.

Forgive Yourself: One slip doesn't ruin your progress. Get back on track with your next meal.

9. The Long-Term Benefits

When you rewire your eating habits, you'll notice changes far beyond the number on the scale:

Increased energy and focus.

Better mood and emotional stability.

Improved digestion and overall health.

Imagine feeling stronger, more confident, and in control of your relationship with food. That's the reward for making these changes.

Final Thoughts

Rewiring eating habits is a journey, not a sprint. Start small, stay consistent, and celebrate every victory along the way. Remember, you're not just changing what you eat—you're transforming your health and your life.

In the next chapter, we'll tackle another key area: how to build wealth by breaking bad money habits. For now, stay focused on making thoughtful, intentional food choices. You've got this!

Chapter 5: Movement as a Lifestyle

Welcome back! We've talked about eating habits, and now it's time to shift focus to another cornerstone of well-being: movement. Exercise isn't just about hitting the gym—it's about integrating physical activity into your daily life in a way that feels natural and sustainable.

This chapter will guide you through the steps to reframe how you think about movement, find activities you enjoy, and develop a lifestyle that supports a healthier, more energized version of yourself.

1. Why Movement Matters

Physical activity impacts your life in countless ways, far beyond burning calories or building muscle. Let's take a moment to understand why movement is essential:

Boosts Energy: Regular activity increases blood flow and oxygen to your cells, keeping you more alert and focused.

Supports Mental Health: Exercise releases endorphins, the "feel-good" chemicals that reduce stress, anxiety, and depression.

Improves Physical Health: Movement strengthens your heart, bones, and muscles, while also reducing the risk of chronic diseases.

Enhances Longevity: Active people are more likely to live longer, healthier lives.

2. Change Your Mindset About Movement

From "Exercise" to "Movement"

Many people view exercise as a chore or punishment for eating too much. Let's shift that mindset. Movement isn't a task to check off—it's a way to celebrate what your body can do and to invest in your health.

The Goal: Find Joy in Moving

The key to making movement a lifestyle is finding activities you genuinely enjoy. Exercise doesn't have to be a workout at the gym; it can be dancing, gardening, walking, or playing a sport.

Your Task:

Take five minutes to reflect:

> What types of movement do you currently enjoy?
>
> What new activities have you been curious to try?

3. Start Small, Build Consistency

You don't need to run a marathon or spend hours exercising to see results. The goal is consistency over intensity.

Ideas for Small Wins:

   Take a 10-minute walk after meals.

   Stretch for 5 minutes in the morning or evening.

   Use the stairs instead of the elevator.

   Park farther away to add extra steps to your day.

Your Task:

Commit to one small movement goal for the week. Examples:

   "I'll walk for 15 minutes every day after dinner."

   "I'll do 10 squats each morning before I brush my teeth."

4. Incorporate Movement Into Your Routine

To make movement a lifestyle, it needs to fit seamlessly into your daily schedule.

Tips for Integrating Movement:

   Active Commutes: Walk or bike to work if possible. If you drive, park farther from the entrance.

   Work Breaks: Stand up and stretch every 30 minutes. Consider a standing desk or walking meetings.

Social Activities: Replace sedentary hangouts (like watching TV) with active ones, such as hiking or playing sports.

Family Time: Turn family time into active time—bike rides, park visits, or dance-offs in the living room.

Your Task:

Identify one area of your routine where you can add movement. Write it down and commit to trying it for the next three days.

5. Focus on Functional Movement

Functional movement mimics real-life activities and builds strength, flexibility, and balance for everyday tasks. This approach is particularly beneficial if you're new to exercise or looking to prevent injuries.

Examples of Functional Movements:

Squats: Mimic sitting and standing, strengthening your legs and core.

Push-Ups: Build upper body strength for tasks like lifting or carrying.

Walking Lunges: Improve balance and leg strength.

Planks: Strengthen your core for better posture and stability.

Your Task:

Choose one functional movement and practice it for 1-2 minutes each day this week.

6. Overcoming Barriers to Movement

Everyone faces obstacles to staying active. Let's address some common ones:

Common Barriers and Solutions:

"I don't have time."

Solution: Break it into short bursts. Even 5 minutes of activity adds up over the day.

"I don't enjoy exercise."

Solution: Try different activities until you find something you love. Movement should feel like a reward, not a punishment.

"I'm too tired."

Solution: Start small. Movement often boosts energy levels instead of depleting them.

Your Task:

Write down your biggest barrier to staying active. Then brainstorm one practical solution you can implement this week.

7. Make It Social

Exercise doesn't have to be a solo activity. In fact, social movement can be more enjoyable and motivating.

Ideas for Social Movement:

Join a local sports team or fitness class.

Take walks with a friend or family member.

Challenge friends to step-count competitions using a fitness tracker.

Volunteer for active causes, such as community clean-ups or charity runs.

Your Task:

Reach out to one person who can be your movement buddy. Schedule a time to do something active together.

8. Track Your Progress and Celebrate Wins

Tracking your movement can help you stay motivated and see how far you've come.

Tracking Methods:

Use a fitness tracker or smartphone app.

Keep a journal to log your daily activity.

Set small milestones and reward yourself when you achieve them.

Your Task:

Pick a tracking method and record your movement for the next week. Choose a small reward for hitting your first milestone.

9. The Long-Term Benefits of Movement

When you make movement a lifestyle, the benefits extend far beyond physical health. Here's what you'll gain:

Increased Confidence: Feeling stronger and more capable boosts self-esteem.

Better Mood: Regular movement reduces stress and enhances mental clarity.

Deeper Connections: Active hobbies can strengthen relationships with friends and family.

Longevity: Staying active helps you live longer and maintain independence as you age.

Final Thoughts

Movement is a gift you give to your body, mind, and spirit. By integrating it into your daily life, you'll build strength, resilience, and a sense of accomplishment that will ripple into every area of your life.

In the next chapter, we'll explore the financial side of breaking bad habits and how to start building wealth through intentional money management. For now, lace up your shoes, get moving, and enjoy the journey. You're doing incredible work!

Chapter 6: Mind Over Plate

Welcome to Chapter 6! In the previous chapters, we tackled the importance of eating habits and movement. Now it's time to focus on the role your mindset plays in your relationship with food. The way you think about eating—your beliefs, emotions, and habits—can either support or sabotage your goals. This chapter will guide you in developing a mindful, intentional approach to eating so you can break free from unhealthy patterns and truly enjoy nourishing your body.

1. The Connection Between Mindset and Eating

Food is more than just fuel—it's tied to culture, comfort, and even self-image. Unfortunately, this emotional connection can sometimes lead to overindulgence, guilt, or restriction.

To transform your eating habits, you need to change your mindset. Mindful eating is the key to making conscious choices that benefit your health and happiness.

2. Understanding Mindless Eating

Mindless eating happens when we eat without paying attention, often leading to overeating or unhealthy choices. Common triggers include:

   Emotional Eating: Using food to cope with stress, sadness, or boredom.

   External Cues: Eating because food is available, not because you're hungry (think buffets or office snacks).

Distractions: Eating while watching TV, scrolling on your phone, or working.

Your Task:

Reflect on the last three meals or snacks you had. Were you truly hungry, or were you eating out of habit, emotion, or distraction? Write down your observations.

3. Practice Mindful Eating

Mindful eating is about slowing down and being fully present with your food. It helps you listen to your body's hunger and fullness signals, making it easier to avoid overeating.

Steps to Practice Mindful Eating:

Pause Before You Eat: Take a moment to check in with yourself. Are you hungry, or are you eating out of habit or emotion?

Engage Your Senses: Notice the colors, smells, and textures of your food before taking a bite.

Eat Slowly: Put your fork down between bites and chew thoroughly.

Listen to Your Body: Stop eating when you're satisfied, not stuffed.

Your Task:

For your next meal, practice mindful eating. Eliminate distractions, eat slowly, and note how the experience feels.

4. Rewriting Food Beliefs

Many of us have internalized beliefs about food that aren't helpful. Common examples include:

"I have to finish everything on my plate."

"Healthy food is boring or bland."

"I've already messed up today, so I might as well eat whatever I want."

How to Reframe These Beliefs:

Old Belief: "I have to finish everything on my plate."

New Belief: "It's okay to save leftovers or stop when I'm full."

Old Belief: "Healthy food is boring or bland."

New Belief: "Healthy food can be delicious with the right preparation."

Your Task:

Write down one negative belief you have about food. Then, create a positive replacement belief and repeat it to yourself daily.

5. Managing Emotional Eating

Emotional eating is one of the most common challenges people face. It's essential to address the emotions behind your eating patterns instead of using food as a coping mechanism.

Steps to Manage Emotional Eating:

   Identify Triggers: Notice when you're reaching for food out of stress, boredom, or sadness.

   Find Alternatives: Replace eating with a healthy coping mechanism, like journaling, meditating, or taking a walk.

   Plan Ahead: Keep healthier snacks available to avoid impulsive decisions.

Your Task:

The next time you feel the urge to eat emotionally, pause and try a non-food coping strategy. Reflect on how it made you feel.

6. Creating a Positive Eating Environment

Your environment influences how much and what you eat. By making small changes to your surroundings, you can naturally support healthier eating habits.

Tips for a Positive Environment:

   Plate Size Matters: Use smaller plates to control portion sizes.

Out of Sight, Out of Mind: Keep unhealthy snacks out of view and place healthy options (like fruit) where they're easily accessible.

Set the Mood: Create a pleasant eating environment by sitting at a table, using proper utensils, and avoiding distractions.

Your Task:

Make one small change to your eating environment today. For example, reorganize your pantry to make healthy options more prominent.

7. Embrace the 80/20 Rule

The 80/20 rule means focusing on healthy choices 80% of the time while allowing yourself some flexibility for indulgences. This approach reduces the pressure to be "perfect" and makes healthy eating more sustainable.

How to Apply the 80/20 Rule:

Plan Your Indulgences: Decide when and how you'll enjoy a treat.

Savor Your Food: When indulging, eat slowly and enjoy every bite without guilt.

Get Back on Track: Return to your healthy eating habits with your next meal.

Your Task:

Pick one indulgence you'll enjoy this week. Plan when and how you'll have it, and practice savoring it mindfully.

8. Cultivate Gratitude for Your Food

Gratitude can transform your relationship with food. By appreciating your meals, you'll feel more satisfied and connected to the act of eating.

Ways to Practice Gratitude:

   Pause Before Eating: Take a moment to reflect on where your food came from and the effort it took to prepare it.

   Express Thanks: Whether silently or out loud, express gratitude for the nourishment your meal provides.

   Enjoy the Process: Savor the cooking and eating experience, not just the result.

Your Task:

Before your next meal, pause and write down three things you're grateful for about your food.

9. The Long-Term Benefits of a Mindful Approach

When you shift your mindset around eating, you'll notice profound changes:

More Control: You'll eat when you're hungry and stop when you're satisfied.

Less Stress: Guilt and anxiety around food will fade.

Better Health: Over time, mindful eating supports a balanced diet and healthier weight.

Deeper Enjoyment: Food becomes a source of pleasure, not frustration.

Final Thoughts

Mindful eating isn't about perfection—it's about creating a thoughtful, intentional relationship with food that empowers you to make healthier choices. By practicing awareness, managing emotions, and embracing balance, you can rewire your mindset and build a lifelong foundation for well-being.

In the next chapter, we'll tackle the financial side of breaking bad habits and explore how to build wealth by transforming your money mindset. For now, keep practicing "mind over plate" and celebrate every small step you take. You've got this!

Chapter 7: Breaking the Cycle of Overspending

Welcome to Chapter 7, where we shift our focus to financial habits. Overspending is one of the most common financial pitfalls. It often stems from deeper issues such as stress, emotional triggers, or even a lack of awareness about where your money is going.

In this chapter, I'll help you identify the causes of overspending, develop strategies to curb it, and create a plan for aligning your spending with your values and financial goals. Remember, financial health is just as critical as physical and emotional health when it comes to overall well-being.

1. Understanding Why You Overspend

To break the cycle of overspending, we must first identify its root causes. Ask yourself:

Common Reasons for Overspending:

   Emotional Triggers: Shopping to cope with stress, sadness, boredom, or low self-esteem.

   Social Pressures: Spending to keep up with friends, trends, or societal expectations.

   Convenience Culture: Relying on impulse purchases or delivery services without considering costs.

   Lack of Awareness: Not tracking your spending or realizing how small purchases add up over time.

Your Task:

Take 10 minutes to reflect on your spending habits. Write down the last three non-essential purchases you made. What motivated those purchases?

2. Recognizing Overspending Patterns

Patterns often drive behavior, and overspending is no different. Identifying when and where you're most likely to overspend can help you break the cycle.

Common Patterns:

   Time of Day: Do you overspend late at night while browsing online stores?

   Places: Are there particular stores, websites, or apps where you always spend too much?

   Emotional States: Do you shop when you're feeling down, stressed, or celebratory?

Your Task:

For one week, track every purchase you make. Use a notebook or app to note what you bought, where you bought it, and how you were feeling at the time. Look for patterns.

3. Shift Your Mindset About Money

Just like with food or exercise, your relationship with money is shaped by your beliefs and attitudes. It's time to reframe those beliefs to support healthier financial habits.

Reframe Common Money Myths:

Myth: "I deserve to treat myself because I work hard."

Truth: You deserve financial stability and peace of mind more than fleeting gratification.

Myth: "I'll start saving when I make more money."

Truth: Saving is a habit, not a number. Even small amounts matter.

Your Task:

Write down one limiting belief about money you hold. Replace it with a positive, empowering statement. For example:

Limiting Belief: "I'll always be bad with money."

Empowering Belief: "I am learning to manage my money and improve every day."

4. Implementing Spending Boundaries

To control overspending, you need clear boundaries for your spending. These guidelines act like guardrails, keeping you on track without feeling overly restrictive.

Strategies to Set Boundaries:

The 24-Hour Rule: Wait 24 hours before making non-essential purchases.

Cash-Only Method: Withdraw a set amount of cash each week for discretionary spending.

Set Monthly Limits: Allocate specific amounts for categories like dining out, entertainment, or clothing.

Your Task:

Pick one spending boundary to implement this week. Write it down and stick to it. For example: "I will use the 24-hour rule for all purchases over $50."

5. Replace Impulse Purchases with Financial Wins

Impulse spending is often a habit, but habits can be replaced. Every time you resist a non-essential purchase, redirect that money toward a financial goal.

Examples of Redirection:

Transfer the amount you didn't spend to your savings account.

Use it to pay down debt.

Invest in something meaningful, like a skill or experience that aligns with your values.

Your Task:

The next time you're tempted to buy something impulsively, pause. Take that money and move it to a savings account or use it to pay off debt. Track how much you're "saving" over time.

6. Align Your Spending with Your Values

Overspending often occurs when your purchases don't align with what truly matters to you. When you identify your core values, you can prioritize spending on things that bring real fulfillment.

Steps to Align Spending:

    Identify Your Values: What's most important to you—family, health, education, experiences?

    Evaluate Purchases: Ask yourself, "Does this purchase align with my values?"

    Plan Ahead: Create a budget that reflects your priorities.

Your Task:

Write down your top three values. For each value, list one way you can adjust your spending to reflect it.

7. Tools to Track and Manage Your Money

Tracking your finances is crucial for breaking the cycle of overspending. Fortunately, there are plenty of tools and techniques to help you stay accountable.

Recommended Tools:

    Budgeting Apps: Apps like Mint, YNAB (You Need A Budget), or EveryDollar can help you track spending in real time.

Spreadsheets: If you prefer a manual approach, create a simple spreadsheet to categorize and total your expenses.

Envelope System: Allocate cash for specific categories and only spend what's in each envelope.

Your Task:

Choose one tool to track your spending this month. Start by entering your expenses from the past week.

8. Overcoming Setbacks

Breaking financial habits takes time, and setbacks are part of the process. The key is to learn from them and keep moving forward.

Tips for Handling Setbacks:

Avoid Shame: Recognize that slip-ups are normal.

Analyze the Trigger: What led to the overspending? How can you address it next time?

Refocus on Goals: Remind yourself of why you're working to improve your financial habits.

Your Task:

Think about a recent setback. Write down what you learned from it and one way you'll handle a similar situation differently in the future.

9. The Long-Term Rewards of Financial Discipline

Breaking the cycle of overspending isn't just about saving money—it's about creating freedom and security in your life.

Benefits You'll Experience:

Reduced Stress: No more worrying about debt or bills.

Increased Savings: Funds for emergencies, goals, and opportunities.

Alignment with Values: Spending on what truly matters brings greater fulfillment.

Building Wealth: Financial discipline is the foundation for growing your wealth over time.

Final Thoughts

Breaking the cycle of overspending is a journey, but every small step you take brings you closer to financial freedom. By understanding your habits, setting boundaries, and aligning your spending with your values, you'll build a healthier relationship with money that supports your long-term goals.

In the next chapter, we'll explore how to strengthen emotional intelligence, helping you build deeper connections and manage your emotions with greater skill. For now, focus on your financial wins and celebrate your progress—you're building a brighter future!

Chapter 8: Building Financial Discipline

Welcome to Chapter 8! Now that we've addressed overspending, it's time to focus on cultivating financial discipline. Discipline is the backbone of financial success—it empowers you to manage your money intentionally, avoid unnecessary debt, and work toward your financial goals with consistency and confidence.

In this chapter, I'll guide you through the practical steps to build financial discipline, helping you stay committed to your plan even when temptations arise. With the right tools, mindset, and strategies, you'll learn how to control your finances instead of letting them control you.

1. Understanding Financial Discipline

Financial discipline is not about deprivation—it's about prioritizing your needs and long-term goals over impulsive desires. It means making thoughtful decisions about how you earn, spend, save, and invest.

The Benefits of Financial Discipline:

Peace of Mind: You'll feel in control of your finances.

Achieving Goals: Consistent effort will bring you closer to financial milestones.

Building Wealth: Discipline allows your money to grow through saving and investing.

Your Task:

Take a moment to define what financial discipline means to you. Write down one long-term benefit you hope to achieve by developing this skill.

2. Setting Clear Financial Goals

Discipline becomes easier when you know what you're working toward. Clear, specific goals provide motivation and direction.

Steps to Set Financial Goals:

Identify Your Priorities: What matters most—paying off debt, saving for a home, or building an emergency fund?

Be Specific: Vague goals lead to vague results. Instead of "save more money," aim for "save $5,000 in 12 months."

Set a Timeline: Deadlines create urgency and help you track progress.

Break It Down: Divide large goals into smaller, manageable milestones.

Your Task:

Write down one short-term (3–6 months) and one long-term (1+ year) financial goal. Be as specific as possible.

3. Creating a Realistic Budget

A budget is your roadmap to financial discipline. It ensures you allocate your income in a way that aligns with your goals.

Key Components of a Budget:

Fixed Expenses: Rent, utilities, insurance, and other recurring costs.

Variable Expenses: Groceries, transportation, entertainment.

Savings: Aim to save at least 20% of your income, if possible.

Debt Repayment: Prioritize paying off high-interest debt.

Your Task:

Create a simple budget for the next month. Use an app, spreadsheet, or pen and paper. Include all income and expenses, and ensure you allocate money toward savings and goals.

4. Practicing Delayed Gratification

Discipline often requires resisting the urge for instant rewards. Delayed gratification is the ability to forego short-term pleasures for long-term gains.

How to Practice Delayed Gratification:

Visualize the Future: Remind yourself of how today's sacrifices lead to tomorrow's success.

Set a Waiting Period: Before making non-essential purchases, wait 24 hours or longer to see if you still want it.

Reward Yourself Strategically: Celebrate milestones with planned rewards, not impulsive splurges.

Your Task:

Identify one area where you can practice delayed gratification this week. For example, skip dining out and put that money toward your savings goal instead.

5. Building an Emergency Fund

An emergency fund is a cornerstone of financial discipline. It prevents unexpected expenses from derailing your progress or forcing you into debt.

Steps to Build an Emergency Fund:

Set a Goal: Aim for 3–6 months' worth of essential expenses.

Start Small: Even $500–$1,000 can make a big difference.

Automate Savings: Set up a recurring transfer to a dedicated savings account.

Your Task:

If you don't already have an emergency fund, open a separate account for this purpose. Decide how much you can contribute each month and set up an automatic transfer.

6. Controlling Impulsive Spending

Impulse purchases are one of the biggest threats to financial discipline. Learning to control these urges will help you stay on track.

Tips to Curb Impulse Spending:

   Use Cash Only: When shopping, bring only the cash you plan to spend.

   Unsubscribe: Remove yourself from email lists or apps that promote sales and discounts.

   Ask Yourself: "Do I need this, or do I just want it?"

Your Task:

Next time you feel the urge to make an impulse purchase, pause and write down the item and the reason you want it. Wait at least 24 hours before deciding.

7. Automating Your Financial Plan

Automation takes the guesswork out of financial discipline. By automating savings, bill payments, and investments, you reduce the risk of forgetting or overspending.

Automation Tips:

   Savings: Set up a direct deposit or recurring transfer to your savings account.

Bills: Automate payments to avoid late fees.

Investments: Use an app or brokerage to invest a fixed amount each month.

Your Task:

Identify one aspect of your finances to automate this week, such as savings or bill payments.

8. Overcoming Financial Setbacks

Even with the best intentions, life happens. The key is to learn from setbacks and adjust your plan without giving up.

Steps to Bounce Back:

Assess the Damage: How much did the setback affect your finances?

Adjust Your Plan: Revisit your budget and goals to account for the setback.

Stay Positive: Focus on progress, not perfection.

Your Task:

Think of a past financial setback. Write down what you learned from the experience and how you can apply that lesson moving forward.

9. Strengthening Your Financial Mindset

Financial discipline is as much about mindset as it is about strategy. Cultivating a disciplined mindset helps you stay committed even when the journey feels challenging.

Mindset Tips:

    Celebrate Progress: Acknowledge your wins, no matter how small.

    Stay Educated: Learn about personal finance through books, podcasts, or courses.

    Practice Gratitude: Focus on what you have, not what you lack.

Your Task:

Each day this week, write down one financial success you achieved, no matter how small. For example: "I skipped buying coffee today and saved $5."

10. The Rewards of Financial Discipline

When you consistently practice financial discipline, you'll experience rewards that go far beyond numbers in a bank account.

Long-Term Benefits:

    Freedom: Fewer financial worries mean more opportunities to pursue what you love.

    Security: An emergency fund and savings bring peace of mind.

    Growth: Investing your money allows it to work for you over time.

    Confidence: Achieving goals builds self-trust and a sense of accomplishment.

Final Thoughts

Building financial discipline is a journey, not a destination. By setting clear goals, managing your money intentionally, and staying committed to your plan, you'll create a foundation for lasting financial success.

In the next chapter, we'll explore emotional intelligence and its role in breaking bad habits. For now, focus on your financial wins and keep moving forward—your future self will thank you!

Chapter 9: The Wealth Mindset

Welcome to Chapter 9! In this chapter, we delve into the transformative concept of the wealth mindset. Wealth is not just about the money in your bank account—it's a way of thinking, a set of beliefs, and a disciplined approach to creating and sustaining prosperity. Developing a wealth mindset shifts your focus from scarcity and short-term gratification to abundance and long-term growth.

In this chapter, I'll guide you to reframe limiting beliefs, adopt habits that align with financial growth, and take practical steps to cultivate a mindset that fosters both financial and personal success.

1. What is a Wealth Mindset?

A wealth mindset is an attitude and approach to life that focuses on opportunity, abundance, and growth. It's not about being born wealthy or having immediate riches—it's about thinking and behaving in ways that naturally lead to financial success over time.

The Core Principles of a Wealth Mindset:

Abundance Over Scarcity: Believing there's enough for everyone, including you, eliminates envy and fosters creative problem-solving.

Growth Over Fixed Thinking: Seeing challenges as opportunities to learn and grow, not insurmountable obstacles.

Long-Term Focus: Prioritizing investments, savings, and strategic decisions over fleeting pleasures.

Taking Ownership: Recognizing that your financial future depends on your actions, not external circumstances.

Your Task:

Write down what wealth means to you beyond money. Is it freedom, security, the ability to give generously, or something else?

2. Reframing Limiting Beliefs About Money

Limiting beliefs about money are mental blocks that can keep you from achieving financial success. These beliefs are often rooted in childhood experiences or societal messages. To adopt a wealth mindset, you must identify and reframe these limiting thoughts.

Common Limiting Beliefs:

"Money is the root of all evil."

Reframe: "Money is a tool that can create positive change in my life and others' lives."

"I'm just bad with money."

Reframe: "I am learning to manage my finances better every day."

"Wealth is for lucky people, not me."

Reframe: "Wealth is built through consistent effort and smart choices, and I am capable of both."

Your Task:

Write down one limiting belief you have about money. Then, reframe it into a positive, empowering statement.

3. Cultivating Habits for a Wealth Mindset

A wealth mindset isn't just about what you think—it's about what you do consistently. Habits are the building blocks of success, and small daily actions can lead to significant financial growth over time.

Wealth-Building Habits:

Daily Gratitude: Start or end your day by writing down three things you're grateful for. Gratitude shifts your focus from lack to abundance.

Track Your Finances: Regularly review your income, expenses, and savings to stay informed and in control.

Invest in Yourself: Dedicate time and resources to personal and professional growth, such as learning new skills or networking.

Learn About Money: Read books, listen to podcasts, or take courses on personal finance and investing.

Your Task:

Choose one new wealth-building habit to adopt this week. Write down how you'll implement it and commit to practicing it daily.

4. Shifting Focus from Spending to Investing

A wealth mindset prioritizes investing over spending. While spending provides short-term satisfaction, investing builds long-term wealth and security. This doesn't just mean financial investments—it includes investing in your skills, health, and relationships.

Types of Investments:

   Financial Investments: Stocks, real estate, mutual funds, or starting a business.

   Self-Development: Education, certifications, or personal coaching.

   Relationships: Building meaningful connections that enrich your life and open doors.

Your Task:

Identify one area in your life where you can shift focus from spending to investing. For example, instead of buying new clothes, invest in an online course to advance your career.

5. Practicing Patience and Delayed Gratification

The wealth mindset embraces patience. Wealth-building is a marathon, not a sprint, and delayed gratification is essential for achieving big financial goals.

How to Practice Delayed Gratification:

   Create Visual Goals: Use vision boards or apps to keep your financial goals top of mind.

Celebrate Milestones: Reward yourself for hitting savings or investment milestones with planned, modest treats.

Remember Your "Why": Keep reminding yourself of the bigger picture—freedom, security, or leaving a legacy.

Your Task:

Write down a short-term financial sacrifice you're willing to make for a long-term goal. For example: "I'll reduce eating out this month to save $300 for my emergency fund."

6. Surrounding Yourself with the Right Influences

Your environment plays a significant role in shaping your mindset. Surround yourself with people, resources, and influences that inspire and support your financial growth.

Tips for a Wealth-Positive Environment:

Join Communities: Connect with like-minded individuals in personal finance or investment groups.

Seek Mentors: Learn from those who have achieved financial success.

Limit Negative Influences: Reduce exposure to people or media that promote excessive spending or scarcity thinking.

Your Task:

Find one new source of inspiration this week—a book, podcast, or community—that aligns with the wealth mindset.

7. The Role of Generosity in the Wealth Mindset

Wealth isn't just about accumulation—it's about using your resources to make a positive impact. Generosity fosters abundance by reinforcing that there's always enough to give.

Ways to Practice Generosity:

Time: Volunteer for causes you care about.

Knowledge: Share financial tips or advice with others.

Money: Donate to charities, fundraisers, or those in need.

Your Task:

Commit to one act of generosity this week. It doesn't have to be financial—time or knowledge are equally valuable.

8. Measuring Progress and Celebrating Wins

Developing a wealth mindset is an ongoing process, and it's essential to recognize your progress along the way. Celebrating small wins keeps you motivated and reinforces positive habits.

Tips for Measuring Progress:

Track Net Worth: Regularly review your assets and liabilities.

Set Milestones: Break long-term goals into smaller achievements.

Reflect on Growth: Take time to acknowledge how far you've come.

Your Task:

Review your financial progress over the past month. Write down one area where you've improved and one small win you can celebrate.

9. The Long-Term Impact of a Wealth Mindset

A wealth mindset doesn't just transform your finances—it transforms your life. It opens up opportunities, reduces stress, and enables you to live with purpose and intention.

Benefits of a Wealth Mindset:

Financial Security: A stable foundation for life's uncertainties.

Freedom of Choice: The ability to pursue your passions without financial constraints.

Legacy Building: Creating opportunities for future generations.

Final Thoughts

Cultivating a wealth mindset is one of the most powerful changes you can make in your life. By reframing your beliefs, adopting wealth-building habits, and focusing on long-term growth, you'll not only achieve financial success but also create a life of abundance and purpose.

In the next chapter, we'll explore emotional intelligence—how mastering your emotions can help you break bad habits, build better relationships, and achieve greater success in every area of life. Keep up the great work—you're on your way to a wealthier, more fulfilling future!

Chapter 10: Understanding Emotional Intelligence (EQ)

Welcome to Chapter 10, where we focus on emotional intelligence (EQ), an essential skill for personal growth and success. EQ is often described as the ability to recognize, understand, and manage your emotions while also understanding and influencing the emotions of others. While IQ measures cognitive intelligence, EQ determines how well you navigate relationships, handle stress, and make decisions—key factors in reversing bad habits and building a more intentional life.

In this chapter, I'll help you understand the components of EQ, how to assess your current emotional intelligence, and actionable ways to improve it.

1. What is Emotional Intelligence (EQ)?

Emotional intelligence is the foundation for effective communication, decision-making, and resilience. People with high EQ tend to manage their lives better, whether in relationships, work, or personal habits.

The Five Core Components of EQ:

    Self-Awareness: Recognizing your emotions and understanding how they affect your thoughts and behavior.

    Self-Regulation: Controlling impulsive feelings and behaviors, staying calm, and adapting to changing circumstances.

    Motivation: Staying driven to achieve goals despite setbacks.

Empathy: Understanding and sharing the feelings of others, fostering connection and compassion.

Social Skills: Building healthy relationships, resolving conflicts, and influencing others effectively.

Your Task:

Reflect on a recent emotional reaction you had. Write down the situation, your feelings, and how it influenced your behavior. Identify which component of EQ was at play.

2. Why EQ Matters in Reversing Bad Habits

Your emotional state often drives your habits—whether it's stress-eating, procrastinating, or avoiding difficult conversations. By improving your EQ, you gain the tools to recognize emotional triggers and respond thoughtfully instead of reactively.

Examples of EQ in Action:

Self-Awareness: Identifying that boredom leads you to snack mindlessly.

Self-Regulation: Resisting the impulse to make an emotional purchase after a stressful day.

Empathy: Understanding your partner's feelings, leading to healthier communication instead of conflict.

Your Task:

Identify one habit you want to break. Ask yourself, "What emotions typically drive this behavior?" Write down your thoughts.

3. Assessing Your Emotional Intelligence

To improve your EQ, you first need to understand where you currently stand. Assessing your strengths and weaknesses in each component will provide a roadmap for growth.

Self-Assessment Questions:

Self-Awareness: How well do I understand my emotions? Can I name them accurately?

Self-Regulation: How often do I act impulsively? Can I stay calm under pressure?

Motivation: Do I set and achieve meaningful goals?

Empathy: How often do I consider other people's feelings before acting?

Social Skills: Do I communicate effectively and resolve conflicts constructively?

Your Task:

Rate yourself on a scale of 1 to 10 for each EQ component. Highlight the areas where you'd like to improve.

4. Developing Self-Awareness

Self-awareness is the cornerstone of emotional intelligence. When you're aware of your emotions, you can understand their impact and take control of your actions.

How to Build Self-Awareness:

   Keep a Journal: Write down your emotions daily and the situations that triggered them.

   Pause and Reflect: When you feel a strong emotion, take a moment to identify it before reacting.

   Seek Feedback: Ask trusted friends or colleagues how they perceive your emotional responses.

Your Task:

Spend one week journaling your emotions. Note patterns—are there specific triggers that lead to frustration, sadness, or joy?

5. Mastering Self-Regulation

Self-regulation involves managing your emotions effectively, so they don't dictate your actions. It's the ability to pause, reflect, and choose your response intentionally.

Techniques for Better Self-Regulation:

   Breathing Exercises: Practice deep breathing to calm yourself during stressful situations.

   Reframe Negative Thoughts: Replace "I'll never succeed" with "I'm learning and improving."

   Set Boundaries: Avoid environments or situations that lead to emotional triggers.

Your Task:

Identify one situation where you tend to react impulsively. Plan a specific strategy to regulate your emotions next time it occurs.

6. Building Empathy

Empathy strengthens relationships by helping you understand and connect with others. It allows you to see situations from their perspective and respond with compassion.

How to Build Empathy:

   Active Listening: Focus fully on what the other person is saying without interrupting or planning your response.

   Ask Questions: Seek to understand, not to judge. For example: "What's been challenging for you lately?"

   Practice Perspective-Taking: Imagine yourself in the other person's situation.

Your Task:

Have a conversation this week where you focus entirely on listening and understanding the other person's perspective. Reflect on how it made you feel.

7. Enhancing Motivation

Motivation is what keeps you moving forward, even when challenges arise. High-EQ individuals stay driven by aligning their actions with their values and goals.

Tips for Enhancing Motivation:

Set Clear Goals: Ensure your goals are specific, measurable, achievable, relevant, and time-bound (SMART).

Visualize Success: Regularly imagine what achieving your goal will look and feel like.

Track Progress: Celebrate small wins to maintain momentum.

Your Task:

Write down one long-term goal and three short-term steps you'll take this week to work toward it.

8. Improving Social Skills

Strong social skills are essential for building healthy relationships and resolving conflicts. They allow you to communicate effectively and foster collaboration.

How to Improve Social Skills:

Practice Clear Communication: Use "I" statements to express feelings and needs without blaming others.

Learn Conflict Resolution: Focus on solutions instead of dwelling on problems.

Show Appreciation: Acknowledge others' contributions and express gratitude.

Your Task:

Identify one relationship where communication could improve. Practice one new skill, such as active listening or expressing appreciation, in your next interaction.

9. The Benefits of a High EQ

When you strengthen your emotional intelligence, you'll notice positive changes in every area of your life:

   Stronger Relationships: Improved communication and empathy lead to deeper connections.

   Better Decision-Making: Emotions no longer cloud your judgment.

   Resilience: You'll bounce back from setbacks with confidence.

   Healthier Habits: You'll handle triggers more effectively, reducing reliance on unhealthy coping mechanisms.

Your Task:

Reflect on how improving your EQ could positively impact your life. Write down one specific area where you'd like to see growth.

Final Thoughts

Understanding and improving your emotional intelligence is one of the most valuable investments you can make in yourself. EQ doesn't just help you manage your emotions—it empowers you to navigate challenges, build meaningful relationships, and create lasting change in your life.

In the next chapter, we'll bring it all together by exploring how these strategies for emotional intelligence, financial discipline, and habit-breaking can create a holistic transformation. You're doing incredible work—keep going!

Chapter 11: Replacing Reactivity with Response

Welcome to Chapter 11! In this chapter, we tackle a skill that can drastically improve your relationships, decision-making, and overall life satisfaction: replacing reactivity with thoughtful response. Reactivity is a reflexive, emotional reaction to a stimulus, often rooted in habit or stress. In contrast, a response is a deliberate and intentional action taken after thoughtful consideration.

Breaking the cycle of reactivity empowers you to regain control over your actions, improve your interactions with others, and cultivate habits aligned with your long-term goals. Let's dive into how you can develop this essential skill.

1. The Difference Between Reactivity and Response

Reactivity often stems from emotional triggers, stress, or ingrained habits. It's impulsive and frequently leads to regret or missed opportunities. Responses, on the other hand, are grounded in awareness and intention.

Characteristics of Reactivity:

Quick, knee-jerk actions.

Driven by strong emotions (anger, fear, frustration).

Often escalates conflict or worsens situations.

Leaves little room for critical thinking or creativity.

Characteristics of Response:

    Thoughtful and deliberate actions.

    Rooted in self-awareness and emotional regulation.

    Focuses on problem-solving and positive outcomes.

    Strengthens relationships and builds trust.

Your Task:

Think about a recent situation where you reacted impulsively. Write down what happened, how you felt, and the outcome. Then, imagine how the situation might have played out if you had responded instead.

2. Recognizing Emotional Triggers

The first step to replacing reactivity with response is identifying what sets you off. Emotional triggers are stimuli that elicit strong, often automatic reactions.

Common Triggers:

    External Triggers: Criticism, rejection, stressful environments.

    Internal Triggers: Self-doubt, fear of failure, past experiences.

How to Identify Your Triggers:

    Journal Your Reactions: Keep a log of moments when you feel yourself reacting impulsively. Note what triggered you and how you felt.

Reflect on Patterns: Look for recurring themes in your reactions.

Pay Attention to Physical Cues: Notice bodily sensations like a racing heart, clenched fists, or tight chest—they often signal emotional activation.

Your Task:

Identify one emotional trigger and describe how it typically affects your behavior. Reflect on why this trigger impacts you and what underlying emotions it brings up.

3. Practicing the Pause

The pause is your most powerful tool in shifting from reaction to response. It creates space for awareness and intentional action.

How to Practice the Pause:

Take a Breath: In moments of emotional intensity, take three slow, deep breaths to calm your nervous system.

Label Your Emotion: Name what you're feeling (e.g., "I feel frustrated") to increase self-awareness.

Ask a Question: Before acting, ask yourself, "What do I want to achieve in this situation?"

Your Task:

The next time you feel yourself about to react, practice the pause. Write down what you did and how it influenced the outcome.

4. Reframing Negative Thoughts

Reactivity is often fueled by negative or distorted thinking patterns. Learning to reframe these thoughts can help you shift your perspective and respond more effectively.

Common Negative Thought Patterns:

Catastrophizing: Expecting the worst possible outcome.

Reframe: "What's the most likely outcome, and how can I prepare?"

Personalization: Assuming others' actions are about you.

Reframe: "This isn't about me—it reflects their state of mind."

Black-and-White Thinking: Viewing situations as all good or all bad.

Reframe: "There are shades of gray—what's the middle ground?"

Your Task:

Write down one recent negative thought and reframe it into a constructive or neutral perspective.

5. Building Emotional Resilience

Emotional resilience helps you remain calm and composed in the face of challenges, reducing the likelihood of reactive behavior.

Strategies for Building Resilience:

Practice Mindfulness: Regular meditation or mindfulness exercises increase your awareness of thoughts and emotions.

Develop Coping Strategies: Have go-to techniques, like journaling, exercising, or talking to a friend, to process emotions constructively.

Cultivate Optimism: Focus on solutions instead of dwelling on problems.

Your Task:

Incorporate one resilience-building activity into your daily routine this week. For example, start each day with a 5-minute mindfulness exercise.

6. Communicating Thoughtfully

Reactivity can harm relationships, while thoughtful communication fosters understanding and connection. Learning to express yourself clearly and respectfully is a key part of responding instead of reacting.

Tips for Thoughtful Communication:

Use "I" Statements: Focus on your feelings and needs (e.g., "I feel hurt when...").

Listen Actively: Pay full attention to the other person without planning your response while they speak.

Focus on Solutions: Instead of assigning blame, work collaboratively to resolve the issue.

Your Task:

The next time you have a difficult conversation, practice using "I" statements and active listening. Reflect on how it influenced the interaction.

7. Practicing Self-Compassion

Reactivity often stems from self-criticism or feelings of inadequacy. Practicing self-compassion helps you treat yourself with kindness and patience, making it easier to respond constructively.

How to Practice Self-Compassion:

   Acknowledge Your Humanity: Remind yourself that everyone makes mistakes and faces challenges.

   Challenge Self-Criticism: Replace harsh judgments with supportive thoughts.

   Take Care of Yourself: Prioritize activities that nourish your body and mind.

Your Task:

Write down a recent mistake you made. Instead of criticizing yourself, write a kind and understanding message to yourself, as if you were talking to a friend.

8. Replacing Habits of Reactivity

Breaking the habit of reactivity requires consistency and intentional practice. The more you choose thoughtful responses, the more natural it will become.

Steps to Replace Reactivity:

Identify Reactive Patterns: Notice specific situations where you often react impulsively.

Create New Scripts: Develop intentional responses to common triggers.

Practice Regularly: Use low-stakes situations to rehearse thoughtful responses.

Your Task:

Choose one reactive habit you want to change. Write down a new script or response you'll use the next time the situation arises.

9. The Long-Term Benefits of Thoughtful Responses

When you replace reactivity with response, you'll notice improvements in many areas of your life:

Stronger Relationships: Others will trust and respect your measured approach.

Better Decisions: Thoughtful actions lead to more effective outcomes.

Reduced Stress: You'll feel more in control of your emotions and behaviors.

Improved Self-Esteem: Responding thoughtfully reinforces a sense of personal empowerment.

Final Thoughts

Learning to replace reactivity with response is a transformative skill that will serve you for a lifetime. By practicing self-awareness, building resilience, and developing thoughtful communication, you'll take control of your actions and create more positive outcomes in every area of your life.

In the next chapter, we'll explore how to sustain these changes and integrate all the lessons from this book into a comprehensive plan for long-term success. Keep up the great work—you're mastering the art of intentional living!

Chapter 12: Strengthening Relationships through Emotional Intelligence (EQ)

In this chapter, we'll explore how emotional intelligence (EQ) can transform your relationships, whether they're with family, friends, colleagues, or romantic partners. Relationships thrive when they're built on trust, empathy, and effective communication—key skills that EQ helps you master. Strengthening your relationships is not just about avoiding conflict but also about creating deeper connections that enrich your life and support your personal growth.

Let's dive into practical strategies for using EQ to nurture and sustain meaningful relationships.

1. The Role of EQ in Relationships

Emotional intelligence lays the foundation for strong relationships. When you understand your emotions and those of others, you can navigate challenges with compassion and clarity.

Why EQ Matters:

Self-Awareness: Helps you understand your emotional needs and communicate them effectively.

Empathy: Enables you to see things from another person's perspective, fostering mutual understanding.

Self-Regulation: Allows you to remain calm and constructive during conflicts.

Social Skills: Improves your ability to build rapport, resolve disputes, and maintain healthy boundaries.

Your Task:

Think of a relationship you want to improve. Write down how the five components of EQ could help in that specific dynamic.

2. Cultivating Emotional Awareness in Relationships

Self-awareness is the starting point for strengthening relationships. Understanding your emotional patterns allows you to interact with others more authentically and effectively.

How to Cultivate Emotional Awareness:

   Check In with Yourself: Before engaging in a difficult conversation, take a moment to identify your emotions and motivations.

   Monitor Emotional Patterns: Notice how certain people or situations consistently make you feel.

   Share Your Feelings Constructively: Use "I" statements to express emotions without placing blame (e.g., "I feel overwhelmed when plans change suddenly.").

Your Task:

For one week, track your emotional responses during interactions with others. Identify one instance where greater self-awareness could have improved the outcome.

3. Developing Empathy for Deeper Connections

Empathy is the bridge to understanding others' perspectives and feelings. When people feel understood, they are more likely to trust and connect with you.

How to Practice Empathy:

Listen Actively: Pay full attention to the other person, focusing on their words, tone, and body language.

Validate Feelings: Acknowledge emotions by saying things like, "That sounds really frustrating."

Ask Open-Ended Questions: Encourage deeper sharing with questions like, "How did that make you feel?"

Your Task:

Choose a person in your life with whom you'd like to connect more deeply. Practice active listening during your next conversation, and reflect on how it changed the interaction.

4. Managing Conflict with Emotional Intelligence

Conflict is inevitable in any relationship, but how you handle it determines whether it strengthens or weakens the bond. EQ helps you approach conflicts with a focus on resolution rather than blame.

Steps to Resolve Conflict Using EQ:

Stay Calm: Practice self-regulation by pausing to breathe or stepping away temporarily if emotions run high.

Focus on the Issue, Not the Person: Avoid personal attacks and concentrate on solving the problem.

Seek Win-Win Solutions: Aim for outcomes that meet both parties' needs whenever possible.

Apologize and Forgive: Acknowledge your mistakes and let go of grudges to rebuild trust.

Your Task:

Think about a recent conflict. Write down how you could have applied these steps to handle it more constructively.

5. Strengthening Communication Skills

Effective communication is the backbone of healthy relationships. EQ equips you with the tools to express yourself clearly while also understanding others.

Tips for Effective Communication:

Practice Transparency: Share your thoughts and feelings honestly but respectfully.

Use Non-Verbal Cues: Maintain open body language and eye contact to show you're engaged.

Avoid Assumptions: Clarify misunderstandings instead of jumping to conclusions.

Timing Matters: Choose the right moment to discuss sensitive topics when both parties are calm and receptive.

Your Task:

Identify one recurring communication issue in a key relationship. Plan and practice how you'll address it using these tips.

6. Setting and Respecting Boundaries

Healthy boundaries protect relationships by ensuring mutual respect and understanding. They help you manage your energy and emotional well-being while fostering trust.

How to Set Boundaries:

Define Your Limits: Be clear about what you're comfortable with and what crosses the line.

Communicate Firmly but Kindly: Use statements like, "I need some quiet time to recharge in the evenings."

Respect Others' Boundaries: Listen and honor what they express as their limits.

Your Task:

Write down one boundary you'd like to establish in a relationship. Practice how you'll communicate it in a respectful and assertive way.

7. Building Trust Through Consistency

Trust is earned through consistent actions that demonstrate reliability and care. It is the cornerstone of any strong relationship.

How to Build Trust:

Follow Through on Commitments: Do what you say you'll do.

Be Honest: Even when the truth is difficult, honesty fosters respect.

Be Supportive: Offer encouragement and assistance without being asked.

Your Task:

Identify one way you can show greater consistency in a relationship. Make a plan to act on it this week.

8. Recognizing and Repairing Relationship Damage

No relationship is perfect, and mistakes happen. The key is to address issues promptly and repair any harm done.

Steps to Repair Damage:

Acknowledge the Issue: Take responsibility for your part in the problem.

Offer a Genuine Apology: Express remorse without justifying your actions.

Make Amends: Ask what you can do to rebuild trust and follow through.

Your Task:

Think of a relationship that has been strained. Write a letter of apology, even if you don't send it, to practice expressing genuine remorse and outlining steps for repair.

9. The Benefits of EQ in Relationships

When you strengthen your relationships through EQ, you'll experience:

Deeper Connections: Empathy and understanding foster meaningful bonds.

Reduced Stress: Healthy relationships provide emotional support during difficult times.

Improved Conflict Resolution: Disagreements are resolved constructively, reducing tension.

Mutual Growth: Strong relationships inspire and support personal and shared growth.

Your Task:

Reflect on one relationship that has improved because of your increased EQ. Write down what you did differently and how it impacted the dynamic.

Final Thoughts

Strengthening relationships through emotional intelligence is one of the most rewarding aspects of personal growth. By practicing empathy, improving communication, and managing conflict thoughtfully, you can create connections that enrich your life and support your journey toward reversing bad habits.

In the next chapter, we'll explore how to maintain all the progress you've made and ensure these changes become lasting parts of your lifestyle. Keep going—you're building a life filled with meaningful, fulfilling relationships!

Chapter 13: Habit Stacking for Success

Welcome to Chapter 13! In this chapter, we'll explore one of the most effective techniques for creating lasting change: habit stacking. Habit stacking is a strategy that involves building new habits by linking them to existing ones. Instead of trying to overhaul your life all at once, you attach small, actionable steps to routines you already perform daily.

This method leverages the power of momentum and consistency, making it easier to integrate positive habits into your life. By the end of this chapter, you'll know how to design and implement habit stacks to support your goals in health, wealth, and emotional intelligence.

1. What Is Habit Stacking?

Habit stacking was popularized by James Clear in Atomic Habits and is grounded in the science of behavioral psychology. The premise is simple: you anchor a new habit to an existing one, creating a chain of behaviors that flow naturally together.

Why It Works:

   Leverages Existing Routines: You're not starting from scratch.

   Reduces Decision Fatigue: You automate the process of building habits.

   Creates Momentum: Small wins compound into big results over time.

Example:

Existing Habit: Brushing your teeth in the morning.

New Habit: Practicing gratitude by listing one thing you're thankful for during or immediately after brushing.

Your Task:

Think of one habit you already do daily. Brainstorm a simple, beneficial habit you could attach to it.

2. Designing Your Habit Stacks

The success of habit stacking lies in thoughtful planning. Here's how to create effective habit stacks:

Step 1: Identify Anchor Habits

Start by listing habits you already do consistently, such as:

- Making coffee.
- Taking a shower.
- Locking the door when leaving home.
- Checking your email.

Step 2: Choose Simple New Habits

Pick small, achievable habits that align with your goals. Examples include:

- Drinking a glass of water after waking up (health).
- Reviewing your budget after lunch (wealth).

Taking three deep breaths before replying to emails (emotional regulation).

Step 3: Write a Habit Stack Formula

Use this format: "After [existing habit], I will [new habit]."

Example: "After I brew my morning coffee, I will review my daily to-do list."

Step 4: Test and Adjust

Start small and refine your stack based on what works for you.

Your Task:

Write out one complete habit stack formula to try this week.

3. Habit Stacking for Health

Creating a healthier lifestyle doesn't have to be overwhelming. Use habit stacking to improve your eating, exercise, and self-care routines.

Examples:

Nutrition: After finishing a meal, I will log what I ate in a food journal.

Exercise: After I brush my teeth at night, I will do 10 pushups.

Self-Care: After I sit down for breakfast, I will meditate for 2 minutes.

Your Task:

Choose one health-related goal. Write a habit stack that supports it and commit to practicing it daily for the next week.

4. Habit Stacking for Wealth

Building financial discipline and wealth requires consistency. Habit stacking can help you establish routines that promote savings, budgeting, and informed decision-making.

Examples:

Budgeting: After checking my email, I will review my bank account balances.

Saving Money: After I receive a paycheck, I will transfer 10% to my savings account.

Learning: After I finish dinner, I will read one article about personal finance.

Your Task:

Identify a financial habit you'd like to develop. Create a habit stack that anchors it to an existing daily routine.

5. Habit Stacking for Emotional Intelligence

Improving emotional intelligence involves practices like mindfulness, empathy, and effective communication. Habit stacking can help you incorporate these practices seamlessly into your day.

Examples:

Mindfulness: After I start my car, I will take three deep breaths before driving.

Empathy: After I finish a conversation, I will reflect on what the other person may have been feeling.

Gratitude: After I open my journal, I will write down one thing I'm grateful for.

Your Task:

Choose an aspect of emotional intelligence you want to strengthen. Write a habit stack that encourages regular practice.

6. Troubleshooting Common Challenges

Even with the best intentions, habit stacking can run into obstacles. Here's how to overcome them:

Challenge 1: Forgetting the New Habit

Solution: Use visual reminders, like sticky notes or phone alarms, to prompt you until the habit becomes automatic.

Challenge 2: Overloading Your Routine

Solution: Start with one small habit stack at a time. Build gradually to avoid overwhelm.

Challenge 3: Losing Motivation

Solution: Celebrate small wins and remind yourself of the bigger goal your habits are supporting.

Your Task:

If you've tried habit stacking before and struggled, identify the challenge you faced and write down a plan to address it.

7. Scaling Your Habit Stacks

Once you've mastered a few small stacks, you can expand them into larger routines. For example:

Morning Routine:

After waking up, I will drink a glass of water.

After drinking water, I will write down my top three goals for the day.

After writing my goals, I will spend 5 minutes stretching.

Evening Routine:

After brushing my teeth, I will review my accomplishments for the day.

After reviewing my accomplishments, I will prepare my outfit for the next day.

After preparing my outfit, I will read 10 pages of a book.

Your Task:

Design a simple morning or evening routine using habit stacking. Start with 2–3 habits and gradually expand.

8. The Long-Term Benefits of Habit Stacking

Habit stacking helps you create a life where success becomes automatic. By linking positive habits to existing routines, you'll:

Save Time: Reduce decision-making by building structured routines.

Stay Consistent: Small daily actions lead to big long-term results.

Achieve Goals: Align your habits with your health, wealth, and personal growth objectives.

Final Thoughts

Habit stacking is more than just a productivity hack—it's a framework for intentional living. By anchoring new habits to existing routines, you can create a ripple effect of positive change across every area of your life.

In the next chapter, we'll bring everything together and discuss how to sustain the progress you've made, ensuring that the habits you've built lead to lasting transformation. You're almost there—keep going!

Chapter 14: The Role of Accountability

Accountability is the invisible force that can make or break your success. It's not just about checking off tasks—it's about fostering commitment, building resilience, and creating a supportive structure that keeps you moving forward, even when motivation wanes.

In this chapter, we'll explore how accountability works, why it's essential for reversing bad habits, and how you can incorporate it into your journey. By the end, you'll have the tools to build systems of accountability that empower you to stay on track and achieve your goals.

1. What Is Accountability?

At its core, accountability is the practice of taking responsibility for your actions and progress. It involves acknowledging both successes and setbacks while striving for continuous improvement.

Key Aspects of Accountability:

   Responsibility: Owning your decisions and their outcomes.

   Transparency: Being honest about your efforts and challenges.

   Support: Leveraging relationships and systems to keep you aligned with your goals.

Your Task:

Reflect on a time when you succeeded because someone or something held you accountable. Write down what worked and how it motivated you.

2. Why Accountability Matters

Without accountability, it's easy to let excuses, distractions, or a lack of discipline derail your progress. Here's why accountability is crucial:

Increases Commitment: You're more likely to follow through on your goals when someone else is aware of them.

Provides Perspective: Others can help you see blind spots and areas for improvement.

Builds Consistency: Regular check-ins create momentum, turning intentions into habits.

Encourages Resilience: Accountability partners or systems can motivate you to keep going during tough times.

Your Task:

Write down one area where a lack of accountability has hindered your progress. Identify how having a system of accountability could have helped.

3. Types of Accountability Systems

Accountability can come in many forms. Choose the one(s) that work best for your personality and goals:

a. Self-Accountability:

Tracking your own progress through tools like journals, habit trackers, or apps.

Example: Use a daily planner to log completed habits or tasks.

Tip: Reflect weekly on what went well and what needs adjustment.

b. Peer Accountability:

Partnering with a friend, colleague, or family member to share goals and progress.

Example: Commit to a weekly check-in with a friend about your fitness goals.

Tip: Choose someone reliable and encouraging.

c. Group Accountability:

Joining a group with shared objectives, such as a fitness class or mastermind group.

Example: Participate in an online forum where members share progress and challenges.

Tip: Be an active participant to get the most out of the group.

d. Professional Accountability:

Hiring a coach, mentor, or therapist to guide and support you.

Example: Work with a financial advisor to create and stick to a budget.

   Tip: Ensure the professional aligns with your values and goals.

Your Task:

Identify which type of accountability resonates with you most. Write down one way to incorporate it into your life this week.

4. Building Accountability into Your Daily Life

To make accountability effective, you need to integrate it into your routines. Here's how:

a. Set Clear Goals:

Accountability starts with knowing what you're aiming for. Define your goals with specific, measurable outcomes.

   Example: Instead of "I want to save money," say, "I will save $100 each week for the next three months."

b. Create Checkpoints:

Break your goal into smaller milestones and schedule regular check-ins.

   Example: Review your spending every Sunday to ensure you're staying within budget.

c. Use Accountability Tools:

Leverage technology to stay on track. Apps, reminders, and digital trackers can help.

Example: Use a fitness app to log workouts and monitor progress.

d. Celebrate Wins:

Acknowledge and reward progress to stay motivated.

Example: Treat yourself to something enjoyable when you hit a key milestone.

Your Task:

Choose one goal and write down three checkpoints to measure your progress. Decide how you'll reward yourself for reaching each one.

5. Accountability in Health

For reversing unhealthy habits, accountability is invaluable. It can keep you motivated and prevent backsliding.

Strategies for Health Accountability:

Track Your Progress: Log workouts, meals, or weight changes daily.

Partner Up: Exercise with a friend or join a fitness group.

Use Professional Support: Hire a personal trainer or nutritionist to guide you.

Your Task:

Set one health goal (e.g., exercising 3 times a week). Write down how you'll hold yourself accountable to achieve it.

6. Accountability in Wealth

Financial discipline thrives on accountability. It keeps you honest about spending, saving, and planning.

Strategies for Financial Accountability:

   Create a Budget: Share it with a trusted friend or advisor.

   Automate Savings: Set up automatic transfers to a savings account.

   Review Monthly: Schedule regular reviews of your financial goals.

Your Task:

Choose one financial habit (e.g., saving $50 per week). Decide how and with whom you'll stay accountable for maintaining it.

7. Accountability in Emotional Growth

Building emotional intelligence requires consistent practice, which accountability can support.

Strategies for EQ Accountability:

   Journaling: Write about daily interactions and reflect on how you handled emotions.

   Practice Check-Ins: Partner with someone to share weekly EQ goals and reflections.

Seek Feedback: Ask trusted individuals for honest input on how you manage emotions.

Your Task:

Write one EQ goal (e.g., pausing before reacting in tense situations). Identify how you'll track progress and who can support you.

8. Overcoming Resistance to Accountability

It's natural to feel hesitant about being held accountable. Here's how to address common barriers:

Barrier 1: Fear of Judgment

   Solution: Choose supportive, non-judgmental people or tools to hold you accountable.

Barrier 2: Avoiding Responsibility

   Solution: Break goals into smaller, manageable steps to make progress feel achievable.

Barrier 3: Lack of Consistency

   Solution: Schedule regular check-ins and set reminders to stay on track.

Your Task:

Identify one barrier you face with accountability and write down how you'll overcome it.

9. The Long-Term Benefits of Accountability

Accountability isn't just a tool for achieving short-term goals—it builds habits that sustain long-term success. With consistent accountability, you'll:

Develop greater self-discipline.

Build trust in yourself and others.

Achieve goals more efficiently.

Create a support system that helps you grow.

Final Thoughts

Accountability transforms intentions into actions and aspirations into accomplishments. By embracing accountability in health, wealth, and emotional intelligence, you'll build the discipline and support needed to reverse bad habits and achieve your goals.

In the next chapter, we'll tie everything together and discuss strategies for maintaining the progress you've made. Stay committed—you're nearing the finish line!

Chapter 15: Celebrating Milestones

You've worked hard to reverse your bad habits, and every step of the journey deserves recognition. Celebrating milestones isn't just about patting yourself on the back; it's a crucial part of reinforcing positive behavior and maintaining motivation for the long haul.

In this chapter, we'll discuss the importance of acknowledging progress, how to define milestones, and the best ways to celebrate them. By the end, you'll know how to make celebration a powerful tool for sustained success.

1. Why Celebrating Milestones Matters

Celebrating milestones isn't self-indulgent—it's strategic. It keeps you engaged, reinforces progress, and creates a positive emotional connection to your efforts.

Benefits of Celebrating Milestones:

   Builds Momentum: Recognizing small wins keeps you motivated to tackle bigger challenges.

   Strengthens Habits: Rewards create positive reinforcement, making new habits stick.

   Boosts Confidence: Celebrations remind you of how far you've come, building self-belief.

   Prevents Burnout: Taking time to celebrate reduces stress and keeps the journey enjoyable.

Your Task:

Reflect on a recent accomplishment, big or small. How did you acknowledge it? If you didn't, consider how you could have celebrated it meaningfully.

2. Defining Your Milestones

Not all milestones need to be monumental. Break your journey into manageable segments and celebrate progress at every stage.

Types of Milestones:

   Micro Milestones: Small, daily or weekly wins (e.g., sticking to your budget for a week).

   Medium Milestones: Significant progress points (e.g., losing 5 lbs, saving $1,000).

   Major Milestones: Reaching long-term goals (e.g., paying off debt, running a marathon).

How to Identify Milestones:

   Align with Your Goals: Choose milestones that reflect progress toward your health, wealth, or EQ objectives.

   Be Specific: Define clear, measurable targets.

   Make Them Realistic: Ensure milestones are challenging but achievable.

Example:

If your goal is to lose 20 lbs, your milestones might be:

Losing the first 5 lbs (micro).

Reaching 10 lbs lost (medium).

Hitting the 20 lb mark (major).

Your Task:

Write down one long-term goal and three milestones that represent progress toward achieving it.

3. Choosing Meaningful Rewards

Celebrations should feel personal and rewarding but not derail your progress. Choose rewards that align with your values and reinforce positive habits.

Reward Ideas by Category:

Health:

Buy new workout gear.

Treat yourself to a massage.

Try a new, healthy recipe.

Wealth:

Allow yourself a small, guilt-free splurge (e.g., a favorite meal or book).

Set aside "fun money" for an experience you enjoy.

Invest in a course or tool that supports your financial goals.

Emotional Intelligence:

Take a day for self-care, like journaling or relaxing in nature.

Celebrate with a friend who has supported your growth.

Reward yourself with time for a favorite hobby.

Your Task:

Choose one milestone you're working toward. Write down a reward that feels meaningful and aligns with your progress.

4. Celebrating Without Sabotaging

It's essential that celebrations don't undo the progress you've made. For example, if you've been working hard on healthy eating, don't let a "cheat meal" turn into a week of overindulgence.

Tips for Balanced Celebrations:

Keep Rewards in Check: Choose rewards that bring joy without compromising your goals.

Celebrate Progress, Not Perfection: Focus on the effort you've made, even if the journey isn't perfect.

Be Creative: Look for non-material ways to celebrate, like spending time with loved ones or exploring new experiences.

Example:

Instead of celebrating weight loss by eating junk food, reward yourself with a new pair of running shoes or a fun outdoor activity.

Your Task:

Think of a time when a celebration led to backtracking. How could you have celebrated differently to maintain momentum?

5. Sharing Your Wins

Celebrations become even more meaningful when shared with others. Whether it's a close friend, family member, or accountability partner, involving others can amplify the joy and motivation.

Ways to Share:

   Social Media: Post about your progress to inspire others.

   Accountability Groups: Share milestones during check-ins.

   Celebrate Together: Invite someone who has supported you to join in your celebration.

Your Task:

Identify one person you'd like to share your next milestone with. Write down how you'll include them in your celebration.

6. Reflecting on Your Journey

Celebrating milestones is also an opportunity to reflect on what you've learned and how you've grown. Use this time to acknowledge your resilience, adaptability, and dedication.

Questions for Reflection:

What challenges did I overcome to reach this milestone?

What strategies worked well, and what could I improve?

How does achieving this milestone bring me closer to my long-term goal?

Your Task:

After reaching your next milestone, spend 10 minutes journaling about your journey so far.

7. The Ripple Effect of Celebrations

When you celebrate, you create positive momentum that affects other areas of your life. Acknowledging progress in one domain (e.g., health) can inspire you to push harder in another (e.g., wealth or EQ).

Examples of Ripple Effects:

Feeling confident after hitting a fitness goal may motivate you to tackle a financial challenge.

Celebrating improved communication with a partner can strengthen your commitment to personal growth.

Your Task:

Write down one recent win and identify how it has positively impacted another area of your life.

8. Creating a Celebration Habit

Just as you build habits for health, wealth, and EQ, you can develop a habit of celebrating progress.

Steps to Make Celebrations Routine:

Plan Ahead: Assign rewards to specific milestones in advance.

Track Progress: Use a journal or tracker to note when you hit milestones.

Schedule Celebrations: Treat celebrations like appointments you won't miss.

Your Task:

Review your current goals and milestones. Schedule a specific time to celebrate your next win.

9. The Long-Term Power of Celebrations

Celebrations are not just about rewards—they're about reinforcing the mindset and behaviors that lead to success. By celebrating consistently, you'll:

Stay motivated through challenges.

Deepen your connection to your goals.

Build a life that values effort and progress.

Final Thoughts

Celebrating milestones is the fuel that powers your journey. By acknowledging progress in meaningful ways, you not only sustain your momentum but also make the process of reversing bad habits an enjoyable and fulfilling experience.

As you move forward, remember that every step—no matter how small—is worth celebrating. In the next and final chapter, we'll focus on maintaining the success you've built and creating a roadmap for lifelong growth. Stay committed—you're almost at the finish line!

Conclusion: Your New Reality

As you come to the end of this journey, you'll have learned the tools to transform your habits and, by extension, your life. But this is just the beginning. The process of reversing bad habits and replacing them with new, empowering ones is ongoing. In fact, the real work begins now. What you've learned can help you create a life of consistent growth, self-mastery, and fulfillment. This new reality is not a distant dream but a reality you can step into right now.

1. Habits Are the Foundation of Your New Reality

The habits you've adopted up to this point have shaped your life in ways both obvious and subtle. They've determined your health, wealth, relationships, and emotional well-being. By changing those habits, you're not just improving individual aspects of your life; you're reshaping the entire foundation upon which your future will be built.

Your new reality will be one where:

Health becomes a habit, not a goal. You won't have to force yourself to make healthy choices; they'll come naturally, embedded in your routines.

Wealth is managed and accumulated systematically, rather than depending on luck or sporadic effort. You will have the tools to make informed financial decisions, save intentionally, and grow your wealth over time.

Emotional intelligence guides your relationships, leading to deeper connections with others and a stronger sense of self. You will be able to navigate life's challenges with grace, empathy, and resilience.

As you continue on your journey, remember that habits compound. Small, consistent actions will lead to monumental changes. This is the power of habits at work.

Reflection Task:

Write down one key habit that has the most potential to transform your life. Describe how it will impact your future reality.

2. The Power of Consistency

One of the most important lessons you've learned in this book is that change happens not in sudden bursts of willpower, but through consistent action. Rewiring your habits is a slow, deliberate process that doesn't always produce immediate results. However, consistency will build momentum and eventually make the behaviors you've worked so hard to establish second nature.

While the temptation to fall back into old patterns will arise, the consistency you've cultivated will become a powerful force that keeps you on track. As you stay committed to your new habits, you'll start to see them take root, becoming easier and more automatic.

The Key to Success:

Don't aim for perfection—instead, focus on progress. If you slip up, simply get back on track without self-judgment.

Celebrate every win, no matter how small. Each positive change reinforces the next step forward.

Track your progress so you can see how far you've come. This will boost your confidence and help you stay motivated.

3. Embrace Setbacks as Opportunities for Growth

Transformation is not linear, and setbacks are an inevitable part of the process. The key is not to view setbacks as failures, but as opportunities for growth and learning.

For example, if you fall back into an old eating habit or overspend, don't use it as an excuse to give up. Instead, use the setback to identify what triggered the behavior, reassess your strategies, and come back stronger. Setbacks are moments of reflection, where you can adjust your approach and sharpen your resolve.

How to Handle Setbacks:

Revisit your triggers: What situation or feeling led you to slip up? How can you address it differently next time?

Practice self-compassion: Understand that change is difficult, and be kind to yourself when things don't go according to plan.

Regroup quickly: Rather than allowing a single slip-up to derail your progress, get back on track immediately and carry forward with determination.

Action Step:

Think about a recent setback you experienced. How can you reframe this as an opportunity for learning and growth?

4. Continuous Growth and Self-Improvement

The work of reversing bad habits is never truly finished. Life is constantly evolving, and as you continue to grow, you'll encounter new challenges, opportunities, and phases of life that require adaptation. Your habits will evolve with you, and the key to lasting success is maintaining a mindset of continuous growth.

How to Keep Growing:

Keep learning: Whether it's through books, courses, or personal experiences, continue to seek knowledge and refine your habits.

Set new goals: As you reach one milestone, set another to keep pushing yourself.

Reflect regularly: Schedule time each month or quarter to reflect on your habits, goals, and overall progress.

The more you invest in your personal growth, the more powerful your habits will become. They'll become a system that supports your ever-evolving vision of who you want to be.

5. The Impact on Others

As you change, so too will your relationships with others. The positive transformation you experience will naturally ripple outward, affecting the people around you. When you embody better habits, you become an example of what's possible, inspiring those around you to make changes of their own.

By strengthening your emotional intelligence, financial discipline, and physical health, you become a better partner, parent, friend, and colleague. The positive energy you create will be contagious, leading to deeper, more fulfilling relationships and a more supportive social network.

Action Step:

Think of one person whose life could be positively impacted by your transformation. How can you share your journey with them or support them in their own growth?

6. Living in Alignment with Your Vision

As you embrace your new reality, ensure that your habits are always aligned with your long-term vision. Your habits should reflect the person you want to become and the life you want to create.

If your vision is to be healthy and strong, your habits should support regular physical activity and balanced nutrition. If your vision is financial independence, your habits should include saving, investing, and budgeting. If your vision is to be emotionally intelligent, your habits should support self-reflection, empathy, and mindfulness.

How to Stay Aligned:

Review your vision regularly: Keep it at the forefront of your mind so you can steer your habits toward it.

Make adjustments as needed: Life changes, and so should your habits. Periodically reassess whether your actions are still aligned with your ultimate goals.

7. Your New Reality Starts Now

You've taken the first step in reversing your bad habits and establishing new, life-affirming routines. The tools and strategies you've learned will serve as a roadmap for your continued success.

But don't wait for a "perfect" moment to begin. Start today. Small actions taken now will lead to big results over time. Each day is an opportunity to reinforce the new habits that will shape your new reality.

Final Encouragement:

You are capable of transformation. The power to change is within you, and now you have the knowledge and tools to do it. Keep your vision clear, your actions consistent, and your mindset open. Your new reality is waiting for you.

Let's make it happen.

Glossary of Terms

Accountability Partner

A trusted individual who provides support, encouragement, and honest feedback to help you stay on track with your goals and habits.

Automaticity

The state where a behavior becomes so ingrained that it happens automatically without conscious effort.

Bad Habit

A recurring behavior that negatively impacts your physical, emotional, or financial well-being, often triggered by immediate gratification.

Behavioral Trigger

An event, emotion, or cue that initiates a habitual action, either positive or negative.

Compound Effect

The principle that small, consistent actions, when repeated over time, produce significant results.

Cues

External or internal triggers that prompt a habitual behavior, such as time of day, location, or emotions.

Delayed Gratification

The ability to resist an immediate reward in favor of a larger or more meaningful reward later.

Discipline

The practice of consistently choosing actions aligned with your long-term goals, even when it feels difficult in the moment.

Emotional Intelligence (EQ)

The ability to recognize, understand, and manage your own emotions while also empathizing with and influencing the emotions of others.

Feedback Loop

A cycle where the results of your behavior provide information that either reinforces or discourages that behavior in the future.

Financial Discipline

The practice of managing money responsibly by budgeting, saving, and avoiding impulsive spending.

Habit Loop

A three-part cycle that drives habitual behavior, consisting of a cue, routine, and reward.

Habit Stacking

The practice of building new habits by linking them to existing ones, making them easier to establish and maintain.

Immediate Gratification

The desire to experience pleasure or fulfillment instantly, often at the expense of long-term goals.

Intrinsic Motivation

A personal drive to achieve something because it aligns with your values and passions, rather than for external rewards.

Keystone Habit

A single habit that has a ripple effect, positively influencing other areas of your life.

Mindfulness

The practice of being present and fully engaged in the moment, which helps in identifying and altering unconscious habits.

Neuroplasticity

The brain's ability to form new connections and pathways, enabling changes in behavior and habits.

Overcorrection

The act of making an extreme or unsustainable change to reverse a bad habit, often leading to burnout or failure.

Positive Reinforcement

Rewarding a desired behavior to encourage its repetition.

Reactive Behavior

An automatic, emotional response to a situation without pause or consideration of the consequences.

Reframing

The act of changing the way you perceive a situation, often turning challenges into opportunities for growth.

Replacement Habit

A positive habit deliberately adopted to take the place of a negative one.

Reward

The benefit or relief that reinforces a habit, encouraging its repetition.

Self-Awareness

The ability to recognize and understand your thoughts, emotions, and behaviors, which is essential for changing habits.

Setback

A temporary lapse in progress that provides an opportunity to reassess and adjust your strategies.

SMART Goals

A goal-setting framework that ensures goals are Specific, Measurable, Achievable, Relevant, and Time-bound.

Sunk Cost Fallacy

The tendency to continue a behavior due to past investment of time, money, or energy, even when it no longer serves you.

Visualization

The practice of mentally imagining your goals and the process of achieving them to increase motivation and clarity.

Willpower

The ability to resist short-term temptations and focus on long-term objectives, often seen as a finite resource that requires replenishment.

Zone of Discomfort

The mental or emotional state where growth and change occur, as it challenges habitual ways of thinking and acting.

This glossary will help clarify key concepts and terms throughout your journey to reverse bad habits and create lasting transformation.

Finally, if you enjoyed this book, please take the time to share your thoughts and post a review on Amazon. It'd be greatly appreciated!

Many Thanks,

Brian Mahoney

www.ingramcontent.com/pod-product-compliance
Lightning Source LLC
LaVergne TN
LVHW012024060526
838201LV00061B/4440